# CHAIR YOGA FOR BUSY MINDS

*Quick and Easy Chair Yoga for Stress Relief, Posture, and Mental Clarity at Work or Home*

Aria Sage

Paperback ISBN: 979-8-9926575-4-8

Hardback ISBN: 979-8-9926575-5-5

For permission requests or inquiries, contact:
The Awesome Readers

https://theawesomereaders.com/

# THANK YOU FOR BEING HERE

Your support means the world to me —
I'm so grateful you spent time with this book.

If you'd like to stay connected or explore more,
feel free to visit my website:

# www.theawesomereaders.com

See you soon,

Aria Sage

# TABLE OF CONTENTS

# INTRODUCTION

Is there a world where you can hold down the job you love no matter how crazy busy it is but stay physically and mentally fit without needing to go to the gym, all the while managing work-related stress to stay sane? The answer is a resounding yes and since you are flipping through the pages of this book, chances are, you are someone who wants to feel better in your body and mind. And you want to do this without pausing your whole workday or getting super physical about it. Well, you have come to the right place. Because this book, **Chair Yoga for Busy Minds;** *Quick and Easy Stretches to Stay Flexible and Stress-Free* was created specially for you.

Most people start their day already behind. They have snoozed alarms, back-to-back meetings and a to-do list that keeps growing before breakfast is even over. Before you know it, their workday blurs into the evening, and by the time it's all said and done, there's barely enough energy left to cook a proper meal, let alone work out. However, underneath all that hustle is a quiet desire to move, to stretch, to breathe. Not just for the sake of fitness, but for sanity. Sound familiar? You want to feel better in your body. Feel less stiff and more energized. You want to reclaim even a small part of your day for you but every attempt at even a basic workout routine feels like another job you don't have time for. Contrary to what you might be feeling, the truth is, it's not about lacking discipline or motivation. It is about needing something that fits the reality of your life.

And for the record, you are not alone in this. So many professionals whether they are in a fast-paced office, working remotely from home, or balancing both worlds, they carry the same secret wish which is to be a little more active, a little less stressed and a whole lot more in tune with their body. Being a busy professional glued to a desk who probably has just enough time to commute between work and home or a remote worker hopping between Zoom calls and other home activities like being a multitasking parent who is trying to squeeze in a little self-care on top of everything else, the need to be physically fit is something that frequently gets shoved down to the bottom of your priority list due to time constraints. And even if you had the time to spare, not everyone is into intense workouts. For those who might be into it, we have already established that a busy lifestyle might not give you enough time to indulge in the desire to get a decent amount of workout into your daily routine. At least not consistently.

This is where chair yoga steps in as an ideal solution and if you look at it objectively , it is not a compromise either. Chair yoga doesn't demand extra hours or expensive gear. It meets you where you are, in the chair you already sit in. So whether you are flipping through this book or listening in, this could be the missing piece you have been quietly looking for as it offers simple, intentional movement that works with your life not against it. It doesn't matter if you have a work life that pushes you to spend long hours in front of screens or you are just feeling stiff from sitting too much, this guide is a gentle way to add movement, breath and balance back into your day without disrupting your current schedule.

The word 'simple' will come up a lot but don't mistake it for easy. In truth, chair yoga is simple yet effective and surprisingly powerful. It is yoga that helps you with your fitness goals right where you are. No need to switch locations or outfits. As the name implies, all you need is a chair, a few minutes and the willingness to pause for a bit. These short sessions that you will find throughout the book are designed to help release tension in your body, improve your posture (which desk jobs can ruin), increase your flexibility and clear up the mental fog typical of most sedentary jobs. The goal is to get you moving just enough to feel refreshed but not become overwhelmed by the prospect of it. With chair yoga, you don't need fancy clothes, yoga mats or a big space. You don't even need to leave your desk. By simply engaging in a few mindful and deliberate movements that are well timed, you can shift your whole energy.

In this book apart from a deeper exploration of chair yoga and how to make it work for you, you will also find;

- Easy-to-follow routines broken into categories that follow the sequence of your day.

- Guided tutorials and clear illustrations to help with your posture and movement.

- Simple tools to help you feel more present, relaxed and energized even on your busiest days.

- Resources to help you get the best results with the limited time you have.

A lot of the chair yoga routines shared in this book are timed perfectly for a quick break with no room to overthink it. This makes you more likely to follow through on your fitness goals. But if you also happen to have enough time for more, you will find something that is perfect for you. Just remember to keep it casual. This book is not here to make you master yoga or get you buff and muscled up. It is all about turning the limited time and opportunity that you have into an efficient tool that helps you look good and feel good. You just need to remind yourself that consistency matters. Even five minutes a day can make a big difference. Chair yoga is more forgiving than most fitness routines but it can still push your limits. So listen to your body. To get the most out of this, you need to make it yours.

Mix, match and revisit the routines you find here based on what your day needs. Keep it flexible. Let the pace be gentle, and the routines are short but make sure you always show up for yourself. If that sounds like a solid plan, then let's get started.

# PART ONE:
## UNDERSTANDING CHAIR YOGA

# CHAPTER ONE
## WHAT IS CHAIR YOGA?

One of the things that probably led you down this path is because life moves fast and your body has been giving you signs that it needs a little care in order to keep up. However, when your career is going at full speed and you find yourself sitting through meetings, answering emails or just stuck in long hours at your desk, it is easy to feel like there just isn't enough time for intentional movement, much less mindfulness. But what if just a few dedicated minutes could shift your whole day? That is what this book is for... a simple, no-pressure guide to reconnecting with your body and breath without altering your work routine or taking you far away from your desk. However, it is important to understand exactly what you are signing up for in order to fully work with it.

In this chapter, here is what you can expect:

- A short history of chair yoga.
- The difference between mat-based yoga and chair yoga.
- The core principles that make this practice effective, even in small doses.
- Real, practical benefits of chair yoga.

Winston Churchill said, *"The farther backward you can look, the farther forward you are likely to see"*, and this perfectly ties into how a deep understanding of something can shape how well you respond to it. Chair yoga isn't about becoming a yogi or squeezing another task into your schedule. It's about finding movement that works with your life regardless of how busy it may be right now. With all of this in mind, let's turn the clock backward and take a trip back to time when gyms and HIIT were nonexistent.

## HISTORY AND BACKGROUND

Contrary to what most people think, chair yoga is not a modern-day shortcut. It actually has deep roots in the centuries old tradition of yoga. Yoga itself as you already know originated thousands of years ago in India as a holistic practice for aligning the body, mind and breath. It was never meant to be only about fancy poses or extreme flexibility. The original purpose was and still is, a way to bring more presence and balance into everyday life. In time, yoga spread across the world and evolved with different lifestyles and cultures. This gradual evolution has had a huge impact on the ways it could be practiced. Chair yoga is one of those beautiful adaptations that resulted from this evolution.

For a fairly accurate timeframe, chair yoga was around in different forms but began gaining more recognition in the 1980s and 1990s. This was largely due to the work of yoga teachers and instructors who wanted to make yoga more accessible to people with limited mobility, older adults or those recovering from injury. But as the practice was slowly integrated into more circles, people started to realize that accessibility wasn't just about age or physical limitations. There were situations where time, environment, and practicality made it difficult to practice. With these hurdles in mind, chair yoga slowly started finding its way into offices, classrooms, and homes. It began taking up spots in places where a traditional yoga mat just didn't fit the picture.

While chair yoga was heartily embraced by the people who benefited from it, you still had some folks who hear the term "chair yoga" and immediately picture something watered down or less effective. It is important to understand that this is simply a general misconception. Chair yoga isn't "easy yoga" or yoga for the lazy. It is smart, intentional movements that use the chair as a tool to;

A. Support alignment.

B. Build strength.

C. Improve flexibility.

And all of this is designed to happen while creating space to breathe. These benefits are just as real as what you get from traditional yoga. You are still activating the muscles in your body, improving circulation which can be disrupted by inactivity and calming the nervous system. The main exception is that you don't need to roll out a mat or get down on the floor.

Chair yoga may have initially evolved because certain people couldn't do yoga the traditional way. But at the core, this evolution happened because yoga itself is adaptable. It is meant to fit or weave itself around your lifestyle. You could be working at a desk, stuck in a waiting room, or at home between tasks but through chair yoga, you are able to tap into the essence of yoga. You integrate mindfulness, breath, movement and presence into whatever you are doing without having to change out of your work clothes or disrupt your flow. So, apart from the chair that is primarily used in chair yoga practice, is there any other significant difference between chair yoga and traditional yoga? This next segment answers that satisfactorily.

# KEY DIFFERENCES BETWEEN TRADITIONAL YOGA AND CHAIR YOGA

First off, let's acknowledge the fact that while chair yoga shares the same roots as traditional yoga, the way it shows up in your day-to-day life is a little different. However, that is actually the point. Traditional yoga often takes place on a mat, with a focus on complete body movements that include standing, balancing and floor-based poses. Typically, traditional yoga requires a certain amount of space, uninterrupted time to be dedicated to sessions and in many cases, a change of clothes or even a whole mood shift. For a busy person like you, meeting this criteria is just not realistic in the middle of a busy workday. On the other hand, chair yoga fits into your life without much effort.

You have the chair that acts as both support and prop, giving your body something solid to work with. By following the movements you learn and merging your sessions into your day, you are able to stay grounded while still engaging in movements that stretch and strengthen your body and at the same time, realign your thoughts and focus. Granted, you won't be flowing into a downward dog or lying in savasana on the floor. But what you will do with chair yoga will be just as enriching. You will be twisting out the tension in your body, loosening those stiff joints that come from lack of frequent use and then using your breath to slow down the mental chaos that a busy work life can create. In short, it is not less yoga, just a different kind of yoga.

Here are some of the other differences between chair yoga and traditional yoga:

# 1. Accessibility and Inclusivity

Chair yoga as previously established removes a lot of the physical barriers that come with traditional yoga. You don't need to get down on a mat, hold weight on your wrists, or worry about balance on one leg. This makes it very doable for folks who have mobility challenges, suffer from chronic pain, are nursing injuries or simply anyone who just doesn't want to twist into a pretzel before lunch. It's yoga that is designed to meet you at your level.

# 2. Time-Efficiency

Time is a valuable currency to extremely busy people. Traditional yoga often needs a dedicated time slot and space among other things such as changing clothes, laying out a mat, warming up, cooling down... chair yoga skips the extra stuff and takes you straight to the point. You can squeeze in a five-minute practice between meetings or during your lunch break, and still feel the benefits. It is efficient for those with tight schedules and real-world routines.

# 3. Integration into Everyday Settings

What fitness routine can you carry out that targets your whole mind and body that doesn't require you to change out of your work clothes or leave your desk? With chair yoga, your workspace becomes your yoga space. You don't need to separate wellness from your day. Instead, what you are doing is blending it in. This makes wellness feel like part of your lifestyle instead of something you have to go somewhere for or another task to cross off your to-do list. This presents a big mindset shift from traditional yoga, which often feels like a separate event.

## 4. Gentle, Mindful Movement Focus

Chair yoga isn't about pushing your body to extremes which let's face it feels like the norm with most forms of exercise. This kind of thinking is further enforced by the no pain, no gain mantra. Chair yoga is more about subtle but controlled movements. The goal is not focused on physique but more about helping you to increase awareness of/in your body, loosen tension that negatively impacts your physical and mental health and building a connection through breath with motion. Traditional yoga can be dynamic and intense but chair yoga invites you to slow down, stay present and work with your body.

## 5. Lower Risk of Injury

Chair yoga limits extreme positions and emphasizes support and as a result, it is less likely to cause strain or overexertion. For people new to yoga or getting back into movement, this matters very much. You don't have to worry about falling out of a pose or pushing past your limit. You also don't have to worry about recovery time after your workouts which in turn helps you stay consistent with your routines. Essentially, chair yoga offers you a safe and stable platform to do things at your pace and still ensures that you get all the mind-body benefits.

Differences aside, chair yoga is built on the same core principles as traditional yoga. One of the most important is mindfulness, which is the ability to tune in, even for just a few minutes, and really notice what your body is feeling in real time. You'd be amazed by how this influences your general well-being in the long run. Then there is breath awareness, which is essential for grounding you when your mind is racing or you are feeling pulled in too many directions. Gentle movement is another key part of this because it reminds your body how to move with ease, even after hours of being still. And lastly, there's intentionality, that quiet reminder that yoga isn't about performing. It is about caring for yourself in a way that is kind, simple, and sustainable. To summarize, chair yoga gives you a way to reconnect without checking out of your day. There is no pressure or judgment. Just a few intentional moments that can shift your energy, clear your head, and make you feel better in/about your mind and body.

## WHY IT WORKS FOR PEOPLE WITH BUSY MINDS

In a perfect world, a lot of us would love to have all the time in the world to hit the gym, go on walks, meditate, stretch, and take long, intentional breaks. But reality dictates otherwise. Between your deadlines, meetings, messages, and the mental load of juggling everything else, that kind of experience feels like a luxury. That is exactly where and why chair yoga shines. It doesn't ask for a change to your whole schedule. It just fits into the edges of it and quietly transforms how you feel, move, and show up in your day. So why exactly is this right for you?

For starters, chair yoga helps to counter the toll that sitting takes on the body physically. When you spend hours hunched over a desk or stuck in one position, your back tightens, your hips lock up and your shoulders creep toward your ears. All of this causes your circulation to slow down. A few minutes of targeted movement can gently reverse all that. You will stretch out the muscles that tensed up from all that sitting, activate your core, release your neck and spine and subsequently reawaken parts of your body that have basically been in "pause" mode during your work day. Over time, this helps to reduce stiffness, improve your posture, and even boost energy levels.

However, the real magic is what it does for your mind. Chair yoga gives your brain the breathing room it rarely gets. By linking movement with breath, you ease stress, quiet mental clutter, and give yourself space to think more clearly. Think of it as hitting a soft reset button mid-day. And when you make it a regular thing, even if it's for just five minutes at a time, you will notice you gradually become more focused, less reactive and more in control of your mood. To top it off, chair yoga is also a brilliant way to stay consistent. Instead of promising yourself that one day you will find time for fitness, you are taking action right now. You don't base your fitness goals on a future event but can start laying the foundation by building strength, working on your flexibility, and infusing some calm into your everyday life right in the middle of your actual routine. No commute, no guilt, no unrealistic expectations. Just small, repeatable practices that support your body and mind in a way that matches your busy schedule.

To wrap things up, if you have ever felt like you don't have time to take care of yourself, chair yoga is proof that you actually do. Just remember that going this route does not mean doing more. It is about doing things smarter. And while the payoff might be a bit slow, it is real. Keep it up and in no time you will experience less tension, better focus, more ease in your body, and a clearer head to tackle whatever comes next.

## CHAPTER TWO
# THE SCIENCE BEHIND IT

It is one thing to say that chair yoga is beneficial but it is another thing to prove that it does. And in a world that is so fast paced, understanding why something works can be the motivation you need to actually stick with it. So now that you know what chair yoga is, the next step is to look at the scientifically backed ways that it actually helps. A lot of people hop on the latest fitness trends in the hopes of getting the kind of results they desire but the problem with doing things this way is that people go into it with a lot of unrealistic expectations and then tend to fall off the wagon long before they reach their goal because reality is different. To avoid that, it is important to know exactly what you are setting yourself up for and getting into the science that explains how chair yoga helps your body move better, your mind feel clearer, and your energy flow stronger is a great start.

In this chapter we explore how;

- Simple movements lead to real physical changes.
- Uncover the mental health benefits that go way beyond "just relaxing".
- Look at what real studies and experts in the field have to say.

Having this kind of information takes away the guesswork from your fitness journey and helps you to set realistic expectations that allow you to become more intentional about what you hope to achieve and how to go about it. Benjamin Franklin said, *"Tell me and I forget. Teach me and I remember. Involve me and I learn"* and this speaks to the idea that when you truly understand how something works, when you are mentally involved, you're more likely to stick with it, not just go through the motions. With this in mind, let us begin.

## How Chair Yoga Improves Flexibility, Posture, and Circulation

When you are sitting for hours, your body isn't just resting, it is adapting. Think about it as setting something in a mold. Your muscles shorten, your joints stiffen and eventually, your blood flow slows down. That tightness you feel in your hips or that dull ache in your lower back? That's your body responding to repetitive stillness. Chair yoga is built to undo exactly that. But is this backed by science or just another bogus claim? Let's delve into things and start by talking about flexibility first. For a standard routine, chair yoga often includes dynamic stretches and gentle 'holds' that gradually lengthen the muscles, especially in the hips, hamstrings, shoulders, and spine.

A 2012 study published in Evidence-Based Complementary and Alternative Medicine found that older adults who practiced seated yoga twice a week experienced noticeable improvements in flexibility and range of motion. Other studies like the quasi experimental study conducted in Taiwan showed significant improvement after just 12 weeks in lower limb flexibility. This benefit is not exclusively for the older generation. Even for younger professionals, these movements help offset the stiffness caused by constant sitting. And the key to achieving this is following through on daily practices with consistency and intention. As for posture, you probably know already that your chair is messing with your spine. Especially since you have to use this same chair every work day while repeating the same movements. When you slouch or lean forward toward screens, the muscles that support the spine get weaker while other muscles like the ones in the chest and neck get tighter.

Chair yoga targets these imbalances and gradually corrects them. Core-engaging poses which you will learn in subsequent chapters strengthen your postural muscles, while openers gently stretch tight areas like your chest and upper back. A 2016 study in the Journal of Physical Therapy Science shows that seated spinal mobility exercises are effective for significantly improved posture and spinal alignment in adults who barely get any daily movement beyond their typical desk or couch routine. This brings us finally to circulation. When you sit still for long, you become prone to numb legs. But it doesn't just stop with the numbness. Reduced blood flow from sitting too long can mess with everything from your energy levels to your ability to focus. However, the subtle movements in chair yoga such as ankle pumps, seated twists, shoulder rolls are able to stimulate circulation without needing you to get up or break a sweat. This spurs an increase in blood flow which then brings fresh oxygen to your brain and muscles. When you have all this in place, you will find yourself being more alert. You will also develop physical endurance. It's like turning the lights back on inside your body.

## MENTAL HEALTH BENEFITS: REDUCING STRESS, ANXIETY, AND IMPROVING FOCUS

For anyone holding down a job whether from home or in a typical work environment, mental strain takes a harder toll on you when you are always on tight deadlines, back-to-back meetings and constant notifications. And it's always easy to be blindsided by how quickly it hits because it builds up fast. Having a mental breakdown is inevitable if you don't schedule some time to stifle the chaos within. That is why one of the most underrated strengths of chair yoga is how it quiets the noise. And the best part is that you can get a handle on things right there in your chair. Now we are not just talking about stretching. This part is about rebalancing your whole nervous system in the middle of a hectic day.

Studies have shown that even brief mindfulness-based movement practices like chair yoga, can significantly lower cortisol, which is also known as the stress hormone. A 2017 study in Frontiers in Human Neuroscience found that just 10 minutes of movement combined with breathwork leads to reduced stress markers and better emotional regulation. What this means for you is that with chair yoga, you can experience fewer anxious spirals, create more calm within yourself and maintain steady focus. The bonus benefit is that subconsciously, your body starts associating your work chair with a moment of pause and relief as opposed to the tension it typically inspires. The 'magic' behind this lies in how chair yoga taps into your parasympathetic nervous system which is also known as your "rest and restore" mode.

Breathing deeply while moving slowly with intention communicates to your brain that it is okay to calm down. That shift without necessarily changing location can ease anxiety, lower blood pressure, and help reset your focus, especially when your mind is scattered or overstimulated at work. The improved focus you experience is a direct result of movement syncing with breath. When your body is engaged in deliberate movement, your mind has something to anchor to. During your chair yoga sessions, you are in your breath, your stretch and your moment. The 10 open tabs and 50 Slack threads no longer take precedence over your emotional well-being. They are still there but your mind becomes clear and your emotions are steady. Even a two-minute chair yoga reset can pull you out of that foggy, distracted state and bring your brain back online.

## RESEARCH INSIGHTS AND CASE STUDIES

Over the past decade, researchers have been digging into the physical and mental benefits of chair yoga, especially for people with limited time, space, or mobility. The results have shown time and time again that chair yoga isn't just a convenient alternative. It is a validated, results-driven practice. One notable 2015 study published in Disability and Rehabilitation observed a group of sedentary office workers who participated in a short, daily chair yoga routine over a time span of eight weeks. The results showed measurable improvements in lower back flexibility, muscle relaxation and posture awareness. Participants in that study also reported a reduction in fatigue and a noticeable drop in daily stress levels. Some were even quoted as saying that the practice became a "mental reset" they looked forward to between work blocks.

From the University of Illinois is another case study where the researchers explored how chair yoga impacted older adults who struggled with chronic pain and anxiety. Impressively, only after just four weeks of regular practice, participants experienced reduced pain intensity and better sleep. But even more reported were the psychological outcomes. A lot of participants mentioned increased self-efficacy, a stronger sense of control over their day and a more optimistic outlook. These benefits weren't just anecdotal. They were backed by standardized stress and wellness assessment tools. But let's look at a group that you might be more interested in. A mid-sized tech firm in San Francisco implemented daily 10-minute chair yoga sessions and tracked employee feedback over three months. Not only did the workers report improved focus and reduced burnout, but HR saw a decrease in sick days and an uptick in engagement scores. One employee pointed out that it was the first time they have felt like they can actually do something for their health without falling behind on work.

It is important to note that these outcomes are not coming from hour-long sessions in yoga studios. They are based on small and sustainable movements built into daily life. So whether you are looking to boost circulation, reduce stress, or just feel more present, the data confirms it. Chair yoga works and it works well. The practices might seem simple but its effects are layered and powerful. What you are really doing every time you practice chair yoga is giving your body what it is built for...movement, even if it is in small doses. And every time you stretch a little further, sit a little taller or feel your fingers tingle from better circulation, that is your body waking back up to its full potential. The physical and mental health benefits of chair yoga are legit and every time you pause to breathe and move, you are rewiring your day for clarity, calm, and control.

# CHAPTER THREE
## SETTING UP FOR SUCCESS

Chair yoga is simple. However, one of the keys to enjoying the benefits lies in making sure that the basic principles are adhered to. The routines and demands are adaptive to whatever lifestyle you have but if you skip on the foundation, you can set yourself up for failure. With chair yoga, setting yourself up for success starts long before your first stretch. It begins with you being intentional. In this chapter, we explore the simple but essential elements that create a supportive foundation for your practice, even when you find yourself in the middle of a hectic workday.

The following topics are heavily discussed in this chapter:

- Choosing the right chair and space.
- How to mentally prepare for chair yoga.
- The power of breath.

Even the simplest practice can deliver powerful results if you are prepared for it. As Confucius once said, "*Success depends upon previous preparation...*" and this rings true with chair yoga. In this chapter, we will be guiding you on how to set the stage without all that fuss so every session you take afterwards feels effortless and impactful.

## CHOOSING THE RIGHT CHAIR AND SPACE

Before you even take your first deep breath or stretch your muscle, setting up your space to create the right atmosphere makes a huge difference. However, don't stress about it. This isn't about buying a new ergonomic throne or rearranging your entire office. You don't need to turn this into an episode of an interior decor based reality show where you shop for things to create the ideal aesthetic. Chair yoga is all about working with what you already have. So whether you have a dedicated office space at home or you are tucked into a cubicle with barely enough room for a coffee mug, you can totally make it work. The main thing is a chair and a space where you can stretch your body while seated without meeting resistance from a wall.

The ideal chair for chair yoga is simple. You want something sturdy, stable and without wheels. Make sure it has a flat, firm seat and a straight back to give your body the support it needs for safe, controlled movement. If you are at the office, opt for that basic meeting room chair over the rolling desk chair. Although, this might mean moving just for a few minutes a day. At home, a dining chair or any armless wooden seat works perfectly. However, if your only option is a chair with wheels, try bracing it against a wall or placing it on a rug to keep it from shifting. You want to create as much stability as possible while you do your movements.

To elaborate on space requirements, you don't need much. At home or at work, you just need enough room to move your arms and legs freely without knocking over a water bottle or elbowing a colleague. A small corner of your office or living room can become your go-to zone. For ambiance, what matters most is creating a mini pocket of intention. This might mean silencing your phone, turning your chair slightly away from your screen or facing a window for a little natural light. Perfection is overrated so don't feel like you have to put up some fancy curtains, get a giant exotic potted plant or any of that jazz to set the right ambiance. The important thing is to make sure you have a clean and quiet place free of distractions.

Finally, let's talk about clothes. While it would certainly be ideal, you don't need to change into leggings and a tank top to get the benefits of chair yoga. The trick is choosing outfits that allow a bit of freedom. This doesn't mean you should ditch formal clothes or skip the company's dress culture entirely. Instead, think soft fabrics with a little stretch or looser fits that don't restrict your hips, shoulders or waist. Go for button-downs with breathable cotton, relaxed trousers, flowy dresses or stretchy office pants. These all work great. At home, you have got even more freedom. Just go for comfort without sacrificing support especially if you will be moving into deeper stretches. That said, if your day involves a more formal dress code, it helps to sneak in shorter practices during your break and save the more dynamic moves for when you are back home and can loosen up a bit.

## PREPARING YOUR MIND: CREATING A RITUAL AND ENVIRONMENT

Chair yoga is more than just a physical reset. There's a mental aspect to it too. Before your body starts to move, your mind needs a chance to pause. Now this can be hard when you are all over the place answering emails, jumping between meetings or trying hard to beat a looming deadline. But even a short practice can affect you differently when you approach it with intention. That being said, preparing your mind doesn't require a silent retreat. It can be as simple as closing your tabs, taking off your glasses, or turning your chair slightly away from your screen. These small shifts tell your brain that you are ready to step away from the chaos for a bit. These little things that you do before you kick off your chair yoga session is what we refer to as a ritual.

Rituals are meant to help anchor you. Maybe you silence your phone, sip a glass of water, or take three slow breaths with your eyes closed. Those tiny actions become cues that you are switching modes from 'doing' to 'being' and this sets the tone mentally and physically. If you are in an office, you might use noise-canceling earbuds with calming music, or just take a moment to face a blank wall or window. At home, you can take things a step further. You can light a candle, dim the lights or even open a window to let in fresh air. None of this has to be perfect. It just has to promote the sense that you are shifting modes.

This ability to shift modes is not going to happen immediately but once your brain gets used to these signals, you will find that you start settling into calm faster. Your nervous system picks up on the pattern and begins to unwind almost on cue. This transition is especially helpful when your days are packed and your stress levels are running high. Think of this prep time like warming up your mind. It goes beyond just doing a few stretches. You are giving yourself permission to reset, recharge and breathe without multitasking.

This ensures that whether your chair yoga time is five minutes or fifteen minutes, you are able to dive right in as soon as your movements begin. Another reason for creating those is that it helps you to carve a little mental doorway into your practice there by making it easier for you to step out of autopilot and into presence. And the more you practice showing up for yourself in this way, the more natural it becomes even when you are in the middle of your busiest day.

## BREATHING TECHNIQUES TO BEGIN EACH SESSION

Breathing is often the part of yoga people overlook but it is also one of the fundamental pillars of yoga. In chair yoga, especially for busy professionals, your breath is the bridge between your racing mind and your grounded body. When you find yourself caught in a crazy work loop that takes you through a series of seemingly never ending tasks, your breath tends to become shallow, fast and stuck high in your chest. That kind of breathing keeps your nervous system in 'alert mode' and this goes on to feed stress, anxiety, and even fatigue. But when you slow down and breathe with intention, everything shifts. Your muscles soften, your thoughts clear up and your body starts to respond with a sense of feeling safe.

Beginning your chair yoga session with conscious breathing helps you shift gears that creates a way for you to step out of the storm, even if it's just for a few minutes. But these short breathing sessions don't just help you to relax. They are there to rewire your system over time to be less reactive to everyday pressure you are frequently exposed to in a work environment. The beautiful thing about this whole thing is that you can literally train your body to handle stress better just by learning how to breathe deeply and intentionally. Let us briefly look at some of the basic breathing forms that can and should be integrated into your chair yoga routine. We are also going to discuss how they serve you so that you can interchange them to match your needs for the day.

## 1. Box Breathing

Box Breathing which is also called Four-Square Breathing is a simple yet powerful breathing technique. It is easy to remember and especially helpful before or after you take on a stressful task. To do this, you simply inhale for four counts, hold for four counts, exhale for four counts and then hold again for four. You can visualize tracing the edges of a square as you breathe. This would give your mind something to anchor to during the exercise. After just a couple of rounds, your heart rate will slow down, your thoughts will untangle and a sense of calm will set in. It's a go-to breathing technique for high performers and first responders and perfect for the workplace.

## 2. Diaphragmatic Breathing

Also known as belly breathing, diaphragmatic breathing is a technique that helps to reverse the shallow chest breathing rhythm we fall into whenever we are tense. To do this efficiently, first you need to sit up tall. Then place one hand on your belly and the other on your chest. Next take a deep breath in. Now when you do so, your aim should be to move only your belly hand. Let it rise with the breath you just took. Then exhale slowly and let it fall. This simple technique is meant to ground you and pull your awareness away from mental clutter. Diaphragmatic breathing is incredibly effective in calming anxiety, which makes it perfect for those times when you are feeling overwhelmed or overstimulated during your workday.

## 3. Alternate Nostril Breathing

Known in some circles as the Nadi Shodhana, this is a technique that is better suited for when you are at home or during a longer break. That is because it is a bit more visually unappealing to any one who might be close by or watching. However, it is great for balancing the mind and settling any mental restlessness you might be feeling. The general idea is to gently close off one nostril and then take in a deep breath through the other. Then for the exhale, you switch sides in such a way that your breath comes out through the nostril that was previously closed. Repeat this pattern back and forth for a few minutes. The result is a smoother and more balanced mental state that leaves you feeling more even and clear-headed.

## 4. Sigh Breathing

This breathing technique is excellent for quick resets during the day, And despite its simplicity, it can be surprisingly powerful. Sigh breathing is exactly what it sounds like. You inhale deeply through the nose and let out a long, audible sigh through the mouth. Repeat this process three to five times at least. What it feels like is letting your body drop weight. Throughout the day, you might pick up some mental load without even being aware of it. This creates a drag that can bring you down emotionally. The sigh breathing technique helps to interrupt stress cycles and reduce the experience of frustration or mental fatigue.

By simply incorporating just a few minutes of breathwork at the start of each chair yoga session, you can draw a clean line between your work tasks and your yoga practice. This allows you to transition faster and smoothly into the chair yoga routines so that you can make the most of it. You mentally signal your mind that you are in a place where you are allowed to slow down, reconnect and navigate your way back to balance. Another great benefit is that you can use these breathing tools anytime, not just during yoga. Whether it is before a meeting, after a tough email or even while waiting for your lunch to heat up, with the proper breathing technique, these seemingly mundane moments can become little doorways that take you to calm, clarity and control.

# PART TWO:
## THE CHAIR YOGA PRACTICE

# CHAPTER FOUR
# MORNING ACTIVATION

Now that you have learned the foundation of chair yoga, the next step is the actual practice. This chapter is all about kick-starting your day with chair yoga moves designed to wake up your body and mind. This can be done even when you are short on time or stuck at your desk. For working professionals, it is not uncommon to get to work in the morning and feel like you have already run through an 80-hour work week. The mental and physical exhaustion can leave you feeling drained long before you turn on your computer. To combat that, we will guide you through:

● Simple stretches.

● Energizing exercises.

● Calming meditation techniques

All of these are designed to fit perfectly into your busy morning routine. With a combination of gentle movement with mindful breathing, you will learn how to prepare yourself mentally and physically for whatever the day throws your way and you learn to do this without disrupting your workflow. After learning different techniques, you will get a full flow session that shows you how to blend these different forms to match your physical, mental and emotional needs for the day.

# STRETCHES TO WAKE UP THE BODY AND ENERGIZE THE MIND

In chair yoga, morning stretches are meant to feel like a gentle nudge to your body and brain that tells you it is time to rise and shine. This comes in very handy whenever you have got a packed day ahead. Right after you wake up, your muscles are typically still in a rested state and your mind might be foggy or already racing through a mental checklist. Incorporating a few minutes of chair yoga can make all the difference as it clears up that mental fog and sharpens your focus. Stretching first thing helps loosen the stiffness in your body, stimulates blood flow and helps to shift your mood from groggy to grounded. It also assists your nervous system in shifting into the right gear for the day.

To make the most of this, aim for that window of time right after you have freshened up and maybe had your first sip of water or tea. Do them before you start attending to screens, emails or the meetings you might have lined up for the day. With even five to ten minutes of intentional movement you can boost your focus, improve circulation and give your muscles and joints a head start. Just remember to take things slow. Stretching should never feel rushed. In fact, none of the routines you learn here should be rushed. Simply open up your mind and ease into it. Here are a few stretch routines that you can mix and match for your chair yoga sessions but first, master the pre-stretch exercise. It works well with any of the stretches.

## Pre-stretch exercise

Position yourself centrally on the chair you have assigned for this purpose.

Allow your body to relax.

Place your palms on your knees.

Visualize a tiny light that starts at the center of your forehead.

Now picture other lights at central locations in your body.

Place one in your neck and another one at the center of your shoulders.

Then place a light at each shoulder point, your chest, both palms, your navel, the midway point between your hips, both your knees, and finally your feet.

Next, visualize these tiny lights flowing downwards towards your feet.

They are not converging but slowly leaving your body and being absorbed by the ground.

This is the tension leaving your body.

Feel your body become lighter.

Take in a deep breath and then slowly exhale.

Repeat until you feel ready to move on to the other exercises.

## 1. Seated Spinal Wake-Up [Spinal Rolls]

First, take a deep breath.

As you inhale,gently arch your spine forward.

Lift your chest and then tilt your chin slightly up.

Exhale and then round the spine backward.

Tuck your chin toward your chest as you do so.

Repeat this wave-like motion slowly and keep up with your breath for 3 to 5 rounds.

Feel your spine waking up, one vertebra at a time.

## 2. Side Body Stretch

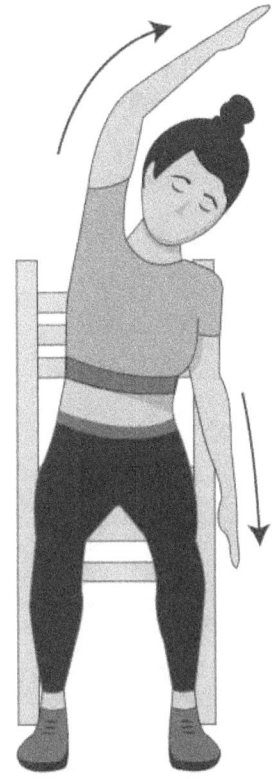

Raise your right arm up toward the ceiling.

Push it upward as much as you can without having to lift your body from the chair.

Take a deep and gently lean to the left as you do so.

Try to maintain the arm stretch even as your hand reaches to the other side without bending.

Feel that stretch all along the side of your body.

Pay attention to the pull from your hip to your fingertips.

Exhale and return to center slowly.

Put your right arm down.

Now lift your left arm and lean to the right and repeat the same movement you just did with the right arm.

After returning to the center, repeat both movements at least 3 more times. Try to maintain your breathing all through.

## 3. Neck Awakening Rolls

With both your palms resting on the corresponding knee, drop your right ear toward your right shoulder.

Hold this position and breathe into the stretch on the left side of your neck.

Now gently roll your chin down toward your chest, then over to the left shoulder.

Do this slowly.

Then hold position again.

Start this slow, neck movement again but begin in the opposite direction.

Repeat as many times as you can or need.

Ensure that you keep your shoulders relaxed throughout.

## 4. Seated Cat-Cow Twist

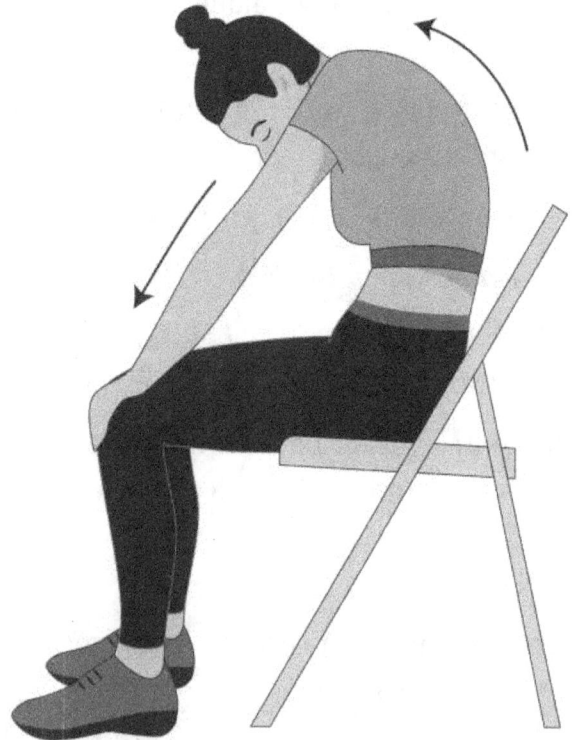

Place both your hands on your knees.

Breathe in deeply and then slowly exhale.

On your next inhale, arch your back and gently look up (Cow).

Then exhale as you round your spine and draw your belly in (Cat).

After one Cat-Cow round, bring your right hand to the back of your chair. Place your left hand to your right knee.

Inhale and do the cow pose to lengthen your spine.

Then on your exhale, gently twist as you round your spine toward the back of the chair.

Hold this position for a breath or two. Then slowly return to the center and repeat the twist on the other side.

## 5. Seated Forward Fold

Place your feet slightly wider than hip distance on the ground.

Take a deep breath and extend your arms up.

On your exhale, slowly nudge your hips forward and let your upper body hover gently over your thighs.

Let your arms hang down to release your head and neck.

Take three full breaths in this position. Feel your back gently stretching and your mind calming as you do so.

Then slowly return to the starting position.

## MORNING CHAIR YOGA EXERCISES

In the morning, your body is typically still transitioning from rest to activity. This is why movements that ground, stretch and slowly activate your energy are ideal. These exercises are usually low-impact and don't require a full workout setup. This gives you room to gently wake up both your muscles and your focus. They achieve this by working to reduce stiffness brought on by sleep, improve your posture even before a long day of sitting begins and create a state of peace within that offers you a calm, clear slate. If these morning exercises are done consistently, they can help to create a rhythm your body learns to rely on. This way, your mornings feel less harried and more like your time.

## 1. Seated Sun Salutation [ Mini Flow ]

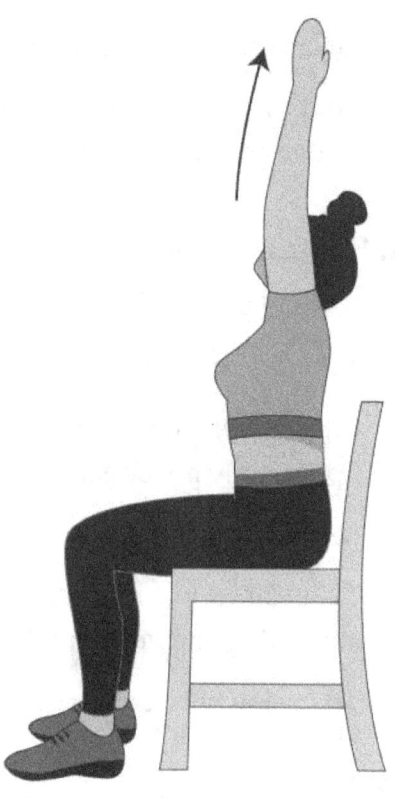

Sit in your chair with your feet flat on the ground.

Take a deep breath and raise both arms up toward the ceiling.

On your exhale, bring your palms together at your heart.

On your next inhale, raise your arms.

As you exhale, fold your body forward over your legs and let your head drop.

Take another breath and lift your body halfway.

Place your hands on shins or thighs but keep your spine long as you do so.

Fold your body completely as you exhale.

Inhale once more and rise back up as you do so. Lift your arms over your head.

Finally, exhale and then bring your hands to your heart.

Repeat this 2–3 times

## 2. Seated Figure Four Stretch

In your seated position, place your right ankle over your left knee, forming a figure four shape.

Sit tall as you flex your right foot to protect the knee.

Then gently lean forward to deepen the stretch in your outer hip.

Hold for a few breaths, then return to start.

After a brief pause, switch sides.

## 3. Seated Cactus Arms Stretch

Stretch your arms out sideways.

Now bend the elbows and open your chest like a goalpost.

Take a deep breath as you push your arms backwards, flexing your shoulders and opening up your chest as you do so.

On your exhale, bring the elbows toward each other and round up the upper back as you do so.

Return to start and repeat 4–5 times after a brief pause.

## 4. Seated Core Twists

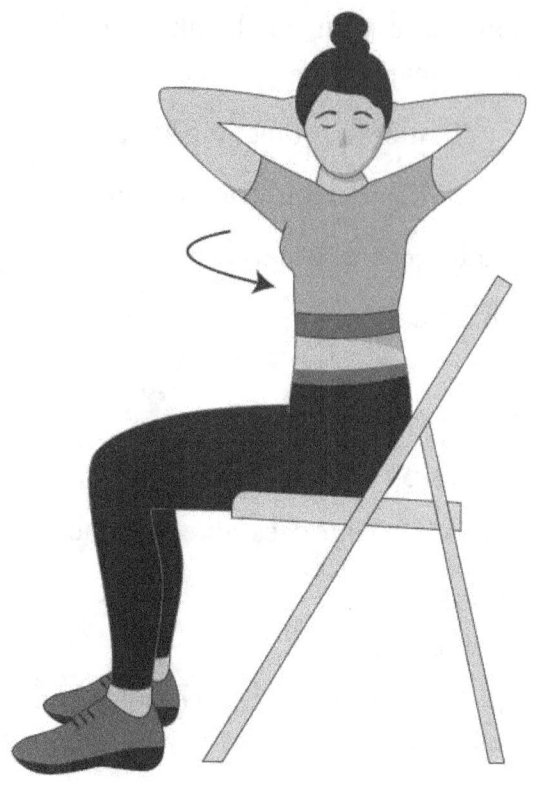

Seat comfortably in your chair with feet firmly planted and slightly apart.

Place your hands behind your head keeping your elbows wide.

Inhale and straighten your back as you do so.

Breathe out slowly and gently twist to the right putting more emphasis on your core than your arms.

Take a deep breath and return to center.

Exhale and then gently twist your body to the left.

Repeat these movements on both sides for 5 rounds.

## 5. Toe Taps with Arm Reach

In your seated position, lift your right foot and tap it forward on the floor while reaching your left arm overhead at the same time.

Return to center.

Then switch sides. Lift your left foot to tap while your right arm reaches.

Keep these movements short and controlled.

Try doing 10 reps.

# CHAIR YOGA MORNING FLOW

For a comprehensive chair yoga morning flow, you need to include breathing exercises, stretch, movement, visualization and some type of manifestation exercise. In this chapter, we have designed a full flow to give you an example of what this looks like. You are encouraged to customize it and make it your own so that you get better results from it. Just be sure to factor in the amount of time you have, where these exercises will be performed as well as how you currently feel.

Sit tall in your chair with both feet grounded.

Close your eyes and bring your attention to your breath

Don't change it...not yet. Just notice it. Feel the air moving in and out through your nose.

With every exhale, imagine letting go of any tension, any lingering drowsiness.

If your thoughts wander, that's perfectly okay. Just gently guide them back to the breath.

Stay in this rhythm for 2–5 minutes, letting each breath anchor you in the present.

Now go into a simple seated side stretch.

Raise your right arm overhead, lean gently to the left. Hold for a few breaths.

Switch sides. Remember to keep it fluid and relaxed.

Next, do a seated forward fold.

Inhale and reach your arms up.

Exhale and then fold forward over your legs, letting your arms dangle.

Feel that release in your spine and lower back.

Come back up slowly, one vertebra at a time.

Next, you transition into cow/cat movement.

Inhale, arch your back, lift your chest and look up.

Then slowly exhale, round your spine, tuck your chin.

Repeat a few times

Return to start and get your body ready for a seated twist.

Take a deep breath and straighten your back.

Then as you exhale, twist gently to the right while holding the backrest or arm of your chair for support.

Stay in this position for 3–5 breaths, then switch sides.

When you are done. Return to start

Next, you will perform a **CHAIR MARCH**.

Start by gently lifting one foot off the ground at a time as if you are marching.

Keep the pace slow and steady.

Then next, add arm raises while you keep marching. Lift your arms up and down but let it be in sync with your breathing. When you inhale, lift your arms up. When you exhale, lower your arms.

Do this for a few rounds and then stop.

Go back to focusing on your breathing as your body readjusts to this stillness.

Once you are calm, take a moment to ask yourself what you need for the day.

The answers may rush at you or you may even draw a blank. That's okay.

Breathe in and with the exhale, verbally set a simple intention.

Something as simple as, "I'll move through the day with ease" or "I choose clarity over chaos, or "I will respond, not react" is perfect.

Repeat that phrase to yourself softly, letting it settle in. This gives your day direction

Still seated and eyes closed, think of three things you are grateful for.

It doesn't have to be grand. Start small. Something as simple as a good night's sleep, your morning cup of coffee, or even just that your internet is working can kick off that sense of gratitude.

Let each item you list bring a soft smile to your face and your heart.

Gratitude resets your brain to scan for the positive instead of spiraling into the stress vortex.

With this new energy, picture yourself moving through your day feeling calm, focused, and present.

See yourself speaking with confidence, flowing through tasks and even taking breaks when you need to.

Breathe into that image. Make it feel real.Your mind is capable of programming you to actually be that person you just pictured.

Now close your eyes.

Sit upright with your hands resting on your thighs.

Begin a few deep belly breaths. Inhale for 4, exhale for 6.

End with one final breath...a long inhale...slow exhale.

Gently open your eyes.

You have just given your body movement, your mind peace, and your spirit some love. You are all set and ready to own your day.

# CHAPTER FIVE
# MIDDAY FOCUS BOOST

The middle of a work day can be a tricky time. You might experience energy dips and your razor sharp focus can start to feel dull. Physically, your body might feel like it has been glued to a chair all day. This chapter is designed for those times during the day when you need to shift back into gear so that you can keep the momentum going. With few and some intentional movements, you can do a total mind and body reset. This section offers;

- Simple and effective midday chair yoga practices.

- Guided flows and innovative exercises.

- Grounding techniques to refresh mind and body.

The primary goal is to help you shake off that slump and get back into flow for work. Even a few short minutes of dedicated time for movement and meditation will leave you feeling refreshed in your body and clear in your mind. This keeps you feeling centered and empowered to take on the rest of the day.

## MOVEMENT BREAKS TO RE-ENERGIZE AND RESET YOUR FOCUS

We have all heard of those crazy midday energy crashes. And despite a crazy busy schedule, your mind still finds the time to wander off track leaving you less motivated and lacking in focus. These gentle movements that we are about to get into are designed to boost circulation, stretch tight muscles. and awaken your nervous system. All three are essential in helping you to shake off sluggishness and sharpen your mental clarity. Just make sure you leave a time slot where you will be uninterrupted for this. 5 minutes is enough to make a big impact. And if you routinely do these daily, you multiply the impact to the point where your body anticipates and responds positively to the movements.

## 1. Seated Shoulder Roll

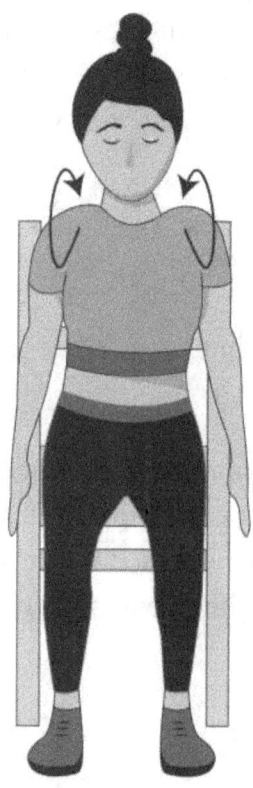

Start by sitting tall in your chair. Keep your feet flat on the floor and a few centimeters apart. Now take a few deep breaths to center yourself. When you are ready, begin with an inhale. As you breathe in, lift your shoulders up toward your ears. Hold for a second and then exhale. As you exhale, roll your shoulders back and down. Repeat this 5 times. This movement helps to loosens tension that builds up from hours of sitting and typing.

## 2. Seated Spinal Twists

Seated spinal twists have different variations all designed to awaken your torso and increase oxygen flow to your brain. It can be adjusted to match your fitness level. But for a standard chair yoga movement, you begin by placing your right hand on the back of your chair. Then you put your left hand on your right thigh. From this position, you gently twist your upper body to the right. Hold for 3 to 5 breaths before switching sides. This movement not only stretches your spine but also releases physical and mental tension which in turn ends up clearing your headspace.

## 3. Seated Spinal Twist with Arm Reach

This is a variation of the seated spinal twist but it works best on a backless chair. You start by sitting tall in your chair with your feet grounded. Breathe in slowly and raise your arms up. As you exhale, twist your torso to the right. Bring your left hand to your right knee and let your right arm stretch out behind you. If your chair has a back then let your arm rest lightly on the back of the chair. Hold this position for a few breaths. Then inhale to return to center, then repeat on the left. Doing this move stimulates spinal fluid, improves digestion, and resets your posture. This is great for both waking up your body and clearing up mental haze.

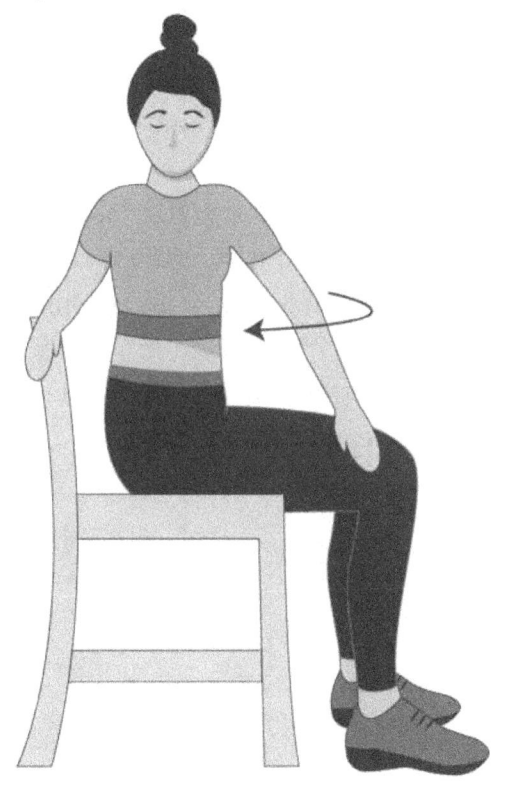

## 4. Chair Eagle Arms [Garudasana Arms]

As with most movements, you begin by sitting upright. Then bring your arms out in front of you. Bend your arms at the elbows and wrap your right arm under your left. When this is done, try to bring your palms together (or as close as you can). Lift your elbows while keeping shoulders down as you do this. Hold position and breathe deeply for 3–5 breaths, then switch sides. This movement opens up your upper back and shoulders, where stress usually sits and causes the muscles to tense up. Chair eagle is also helpful with focus and coordination.

## MIDDAY CHAIR YOGA EXERCISES

With a few exceptions here and there, it is a given that by midday, most people are running on mental fumes. Between juggling deadlines, office politics and screen overload, your mind becomes scattered, your body stiffens, and stress quietly takes the wheel. This causes a dip in energy and focus even when there is still so much work left to do. These midday chair yoga exercises we are about to share provide a form of reset to help you shake off that mental clutter, recharge your energy and return to your tasks with a clearer head.

## Seated Eagle Legs with Arm Wrap.

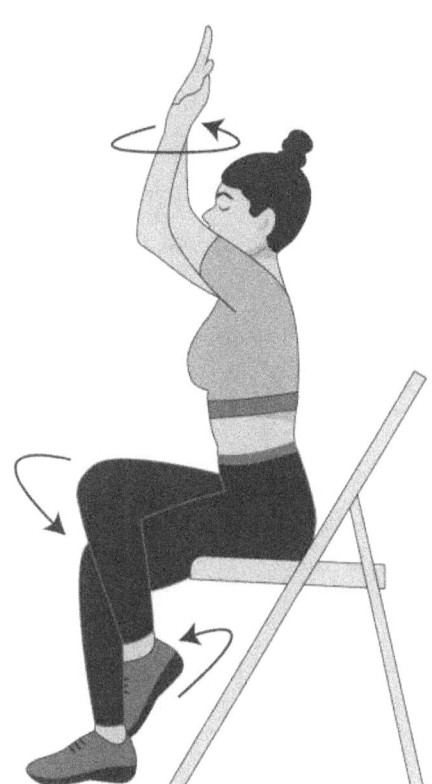

Sit tall and straight in your chair. Now cross your right leg over your left thigh. Flex your right foot in a way that helps it stay protectively on your left knee. Pay attention to your body as you perform this move because you might be pushing your limits a little with this. Now, cross your arms at the elbows and wrap your forearms. For an extension of this exercise, try pressing your palms together. Hold this position for 5 slow breaths. Then switch legs and repeat. This move is designed to open tight hips and shoulders and release built-up tension while improving your focus.

## Seated Figure Four Stretch.

In a seated position, place your right ankle gently over your left thigh just above the knee. Keep your back tall and straight. Now bend forward slightly. You will feel a stretch deep in your hip. You can hold the sides of the chair for support if your body is still just getting used to this position. Continue your bend and keep pushing forward until you reach that point where your whole body looks like the number 4. Hold here for 5 deep breaths, then switch sides and repeat. This exercise is great for loosening your hips and easing any lower back tightness you might feel from hours of sitting.

## Chair Pigeon Twist

Get into this position by crossing your right ankle over your left thigh. Keep your back straight and your chin up. From this position, place your left hand on the outside of your right knee. Then twist your upper body gently to the right. Now look over your right shoulder without and hold while you gently breathe into the twist. Do this for 5 breaths. Return to the starting position, switch to placing your left ankle over your right thigh and then repeat the routine. Doing this combination opens up your hips and massages your spine, and it is designed to wake up your whole core.

## Seated Side Bend with Arm Reach

This chair yoga move is perfect for a little pick-me-up in the middle of a very busy work day. First, sit with your feet flat and your back straight. Then take a deep inhale and lift your right arm up and over your head. Lean gently to the left as you do. You can keep your left hand resting lightly on your chair for support. Go deep into the side body stretch and breathe deep for 5 breaths. Then switch sides and repeat. This stretch expands your rib cage and helps to stimulate deep breathing which does a great job of clearing out mental cobwebs.

## Seated Leg Extensions with Toe Flex

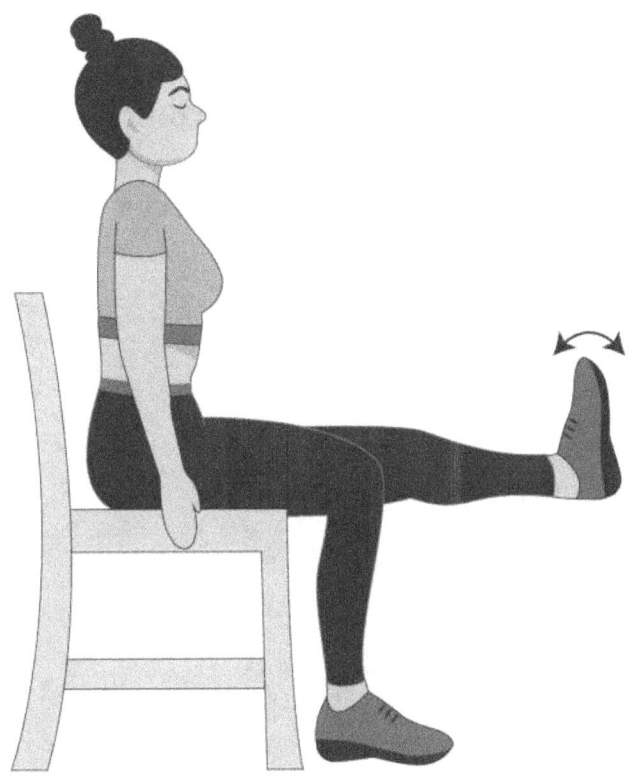

This is a simple stretch exercise that can be done at any time. Not just during your midday session. Start by sitting straight and tall in your chair. Next, lift your right leg straight out in front of you. Now, flex your toes toward you. Go as far as your toes can go. Hold this position for 10 seconds and then point your toes in the opposite direction which is away from you and hold for another 10 seconds. Lower your leg and repeat the same movements with your left leg. Aim to do 8 reps each side. This movement awakens your legs and improves circulation which is perfect for those days when you do a lot of sitting down.

## Creating a Midday Flow for Energy Boost

By the time you get to the middle of your day, you will find that your attention span has waned and exhaustion has already started to creep in. Your body will also starting showing signs of stiffness. A midday session can call you energy back to you, realign your focus and help you feel rejuvenated. A combination of some of the midday exercises combined with some stretches and meditation forms can put you in the right frame of mind to get you through the rest of the day. Here's a sample of what your midday chair yoga session can look like. You can use this as it or mix and match to suit the needs of your body.

To begin, take a deep breath in...

Let it fill up your chest and then gently let it go.

Remind yourself that this moment has been carved out just for you.

Allow that knowledge fill you with warmth.

Take a few more deep breaths and you are ready to dive in deeper.

Now sit tall in your chair with your feet flat on the floor.

Let your hands rest lightly on your thighs.

Close your eyes and imagine a string gently pulling you up from the crown of your head.

Feel your spine straighten and lengthen every time this imaginary thread is pulled upward.

Relax and release your body.

On your next inhale, Roll your shoulders up... take it back... and then roll back down.

Let's begin with a seated side bend.

Take a deep breath.

Now lift your right arm up toward the ceiling in a slow swing motion.

As you exhale, gently lean to the left and stretch your side body as you do so.

Stay here for three deep breaths.

Inhale as you come back up. Exhale and feel the tension leaving your body.

Now switch sides.

Inhale as your left arm rises. Exhale as you bend and stretch to the right.


Lean deep into that stretch and then feel the release. Let the breath guide you back to the initial seated position.

Now, we move to the seated figure four stretch.

Make sure you are sitting up tall.

Now put your right ankle over your left thigh.

When you are good and comfortable, hinge forward just a little while keeping your back long.

Breathe in this position for five full breaths.

Pay attention to where you are holding tension. This could be in your in your hips, your back and/or your jaw.

When you pinpoint your tension spot, release and let it go with each exhale.

Gently return to your start position and switch legs.

You are doing good. Now, it is time to build into movement.

Place both your feet firmly to the floor.

Inhale, let your arms sweep out and then up.

Exhale and bend your elbows out to the sides. Lift your chest as you do so.

Feel your chest open and shoulders draw back.

Take your hands down and then do this movement two more times. Inhale as you reach up. Exhale as you open wide.

Return to your start position. Keep your breaths deep and even. Let's build this with a seated eagle stretch.

First, cross your right leg over your left leg. Then wrap your right arm under your left arm.

Settle into this position before bringing your palms together [if you can].

Your elbows might lift just a little. Sit in this position keeping your body tall and straight.

Take a deep breath...exhale slowly.

Take four more deep breaths and then slowly unwrap your body and switch sides.

Repeat this this twice and then transition into seated leg extension.

In your primary start position, extend your right leg out. Point your toes towards you and then away from you a few times.

Lower your leg down and then switch sides. Do the same with the left.

If your chair is steady and you feel up to it, do this toe stretch movement with both legs up at the same time.

This will activate your thighs and core. Get more out of this exercise by holding for a few breaths before you release.

Now that you have gotten some movement in, it is time to transition softly to stillness.

Sit up straight and place your hands gently on your lap.

Close your eyes and come back to your breath. Inhale through the nose... exhale slowly through the mouth.

Observe how your body feels as you breathe this way. Feel yourself become lighter and calmer.

For the next minute, let your focus be on this quiet space.

If you feel your mind drifting, that's okay. Just return to your breath. Inhale... and exhale.

Let these breaths be your anchor.

Now slowly open your eyes.


Give your shoulders one last roll back. Gift yourself a soft smile. You showed up. You reset. You are ready for the rest of your day.

# CHAPTER SIX
## EVENING WIND-DOWN

This chapter is all about creating a space that equips you to let go. After a full day of demands related to work and/or other equally demanding areas of your life, movement as you unwind becomes less about productivity and more about release. In this chapter, you will be introduced to gentle chair yoga practices designed to ease your body and calm your mind. It offers you a smooth transition from work mode into rest mode. Some of the things you will get here include:

- Intentional movements ranging from shoulder sweeps to seated folds.

- Deliberate actions you can take to create cues that prompts you to rest.

- Specific exercises that help you to shake off screen-time tension, loosen up tight muscles and mentally disconnect from the noise of the day.

Whether you have only got ten minutes after shutting down your laptop or you are hoping to follow through on the desire to carve out a longer evening ritual, the wind-down chair yoga flow session in this chapter gives you the necessary tools to decompress fully. Something you will appreciate is your exploration of soft movements, grounding breathwork and quiet moments of meditation that invite restfulness from the inside out. Combining the session with the right atmosphere (think dim lights, calming sounds or even a warm cup of tea) turns this practice into something that becomes more than just a stretch.

## DECOMPRESS FROM SCREEN TIME AND STRESS

To successfully detach yourself from everything that went on in your work day, you have to first acknowledge that your evenings are sacred, not a time to catch up on work you missed. You must learn to treat your evenings as a soft landing zone that you enter into after the nonstop buzz of the workday. This clear mental separation can help you transition easily into a quiet home life that nurtures your mind and body. However, it is difficult for most people, to make this separation especially if they work from home to begin with. Just as you log off your last meeting, you rub your eyes and realize your body has been locked in the same position for hours. This puts you in a post-work mode that doesn't quite feel like home.

Your mind is probably still racing so you might still be in "go mode" particularly if you had a stressful day. It is not uncommon to find yourself replaying conversations, mentally documenting your unfinished tasks and making a list of tomorrow's worries. You have turned off your screen and maybe even left your office but you mind is still in work mode albeit the unproductive side of it. This is an evening chair yoga flow steps in. Try not to think of it as another task on your list but as a gentle signal to your mind and body that you can let go now. But it is not always easy to jump into a session when your mind is still working through the kinks and lows of your work day. However, there are things you can do to switch off completely.

## 1. Start With Intention.

A good evening wind-down session starts with intention. After a busy day, it's to going take more than willpower to turn things off. You need to set cues that can act as mental prompts. These cues set the tone so you must be intentional about them. Find a quiet corner in your home. Dim the lights if you can. If not, be sure to get rid or turn off any harsh overhead glare. Settle in nicely into this corner. Add a cozy touch to help you ease out of work mode. A nice hot cup of herbal tea, soft instrumental music playing in the background or even a calming scent like lavender or eucalyptus are excellent additions to your cozy corner. When you settle into your chair, close your eyes and take a few slow, deep breaths. Let the breath be your cue to stop carrying the day.

## 2. Engage in Small Deliberate Movements

Resist the urge to go into sleep right away. You need to get some movements in before that happens. That said, chair yoga at this time is all about soft, restorative movements. Think gentle neck rolls to release screen-time tension, shoulder shrugs and circles to melt away stress and then forward folds that invite your nervous system to relax. You can add in a few twists to ease spinal tension and seated cat-cow stretches to help the body remember how to move freely again. You don't want to make it about stretching far. The focus should be more on letting your breath guide your body back to ease.

## 3. Finish With Meditation

For a complete post-work chair yoga session, ending with a moment of stillness or a short guided meditation is essential to help seal the session. As you know, meditation comes in different forms. You can simply ket yourself just sit, breathe, and feel. The main purpose of doing yoga at this time is not to accomplish something grand or hit some body milestone. You are doing it to unwind, to transition and to return to yourself after giving so much of your energy away all day. Just by putting a few intentional minutes packed with some movements and routines like the ones mentioned here can shift the entire mood of your evening. This will help you sleep better, feel lighter and equip you to face the next day with more calm than chaos.

## CHAIR YOGA EXERCISES TO DECOMPRESS

After you have been through a long day of deadlines, endless screen time and nonstop mental load, your body craves a release from all of this. Beyond that, your mind needs permission to slow down and rest. This next set of gentle chair yoga exercises prioritizes these needs as they are designed to help you decompress fully. At the end of your session, you should be able to leave the day behind and then shift into a more restful and grounded state. Each movement is simple yet purposeful. You should be able to ease the tension that builds up in the wrists, shoulders, back, and mind. Think of these exercises as your bridge between the busy energy of the workday and the calm you deserve at night. You want to be able to rest deeper when you sleep, feel better when you wake up and then show up fresh the next day.

# 1. Seated Shoulder Sweep

Sit tall in your chair with your hands resting on your thighs. Take a deep breath and then do a slow upward sweeping motion with your arms till they are fully up and right above your head. The sweeping motion should be straight and outward from your body. When your hands are up, let your fingers lightly touch each other. Now exhale as you slowly lower your arms in a wide arc back down to your sides. Try to keep your palms facing down. Repeat this movement 4 – 5 times. Keep your movements slow and smooth. This movement opens your chest, relieves any shoulder tension you might feel and then slows your breathing. It is particularly suited for letting go of screen induced stress.

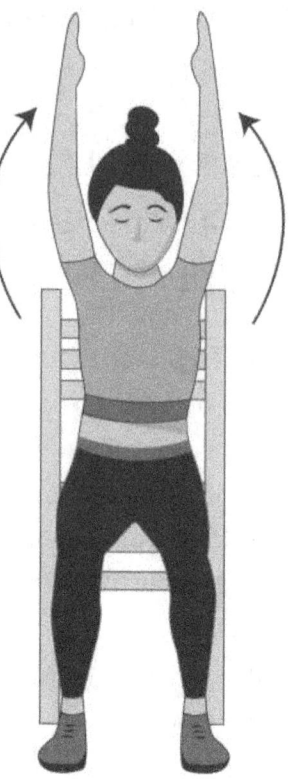

# 2. Gentle Wrist Rolls and Finger Stretch

Sit up straight in your chair. Now, extend your arms forward until they are at your shoulder height. Keeping your body and arms straight, gently rotate your wrists in slow circles. First do this clockwise. Then proceed to move them counterclockwise. After a few rounds of this repeated motion, stretch your fingers wide. Imagine that you are shaking off the day as you do so. Then make a loose fist and release. Repeat several times and then put your hands down. Since so much of your day is typically spent typing, clicking, texting, this subtle move helps to release tension from those overused hands and wrists. The main purpose is to promote full-body relaxation.

## 3. Seated Side Stretch with Neck Drop

From your primary start position, place your right hand on the seat beside you. Now take a deep breath and reach your left arm overhead. Do a straight gentle stretch to the right. While you are in this stretch, let your head drop softly toward your right shoulder. Lean into this stretch as far as your body will allow and then hold this position for a few breaths. Return to your start position as you exhale and then switch sides. This movement releases tension from your neck, shoulders and the sides of your torso. These are prime areas that carry stress from all that sitting, typing and thinking that you tend to do all day at work.

## 4. Forward Fold with Arm Hang

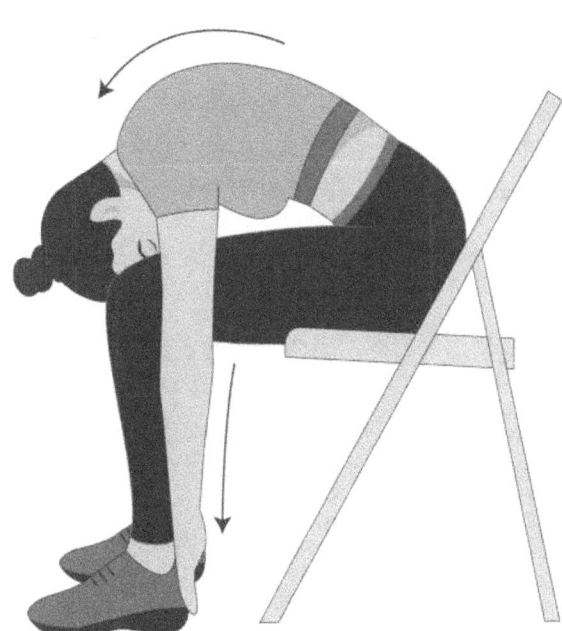

This is a go-to move that almost instantly destresses you. And just like all the moves in this segment, it is so easy to get into. Start by sitting on the edge of your chair. Keep your feet flat on the ground and spread out wide. Next, inhale deeply. As you draw that deep breath, slowly fold your body forward from your hips. Let your torso drape over your thighs and your arms hang down toward the floor. Let your head hang completely. Stay in this position for about 5–10 deep breaths. This inversion is very helpful for calming your nervous system while reducing any lower back pressure. It also is effective at shifting your mental pace from active to restful.

## 5. Seated Eye Palming

This move is not your typical chair yoga move but it plays very well into simple cues you can use to teach your body and mind to calm down and unwind. It is also something you can quickly do in the middle of your work day or those days when you are super engaged with your screen. To do this move, simply rub your palms together until they feel warm. Next, gently cup your warm palms over your closed eyes without pressing down. Breathe deeply and sit in the darkness for about 30 seconds to 1 minute at a time. This move is effective for soothing your eyes. It also has the same effect on your nervous system. The heat you generate through the palm friction helps to release screen strain, reduce tension headaches and when paired with deep breathing, it creates an instant feeling of peace.

## A FULL CHAIR YOGA WIND-DOWN FLOW

Take yourself to your space for this session. Set the ambience for your relaxation. Whether that is scented candles or just soft lights, calming scents or sounds, choose what really makes you feel at ease. Take this time just for you. Here, there are no deadlines, no pressure, no work. Just a slow and intentional return to calm. Welcome to your evening reset.

Sit comfortably in your chair with both feet planted firmly on the ground.

Close your eyes. Now take a slow, deep breath in through your nose...lift your shoulders as the air fills up your chest cavity.

Exhale fully through your mouth. Let your shoulders drop as you feel the air coming out.

Do this again. Take a deep breath, filling your belly with air...

Exhale and then soften your jaw and your forehead.

Repeat this process for a few rounds. Let your breath settle into a gentle rhythm.

When you feel yourself becoming in sync with your breathing, slowly, sweep both arms overhead on your next inhale.

Hold for a few seconds and when you exhale, lower your arms in a wide arc back down to your sides.

Repeat this move 4 more times. Ensure that your movement is in sync with your breathing.

Every time you exhale, imagine your body releasing the weight of the day.

After your fourth movement, pause your movements for a few more breaths with your arms and the rest of your body relaxed.

You can pause here for a moment and just embrace what you are experiencing right now.

When you feel ready, extend both of your arms in front of you. Then, roll your wrists in slow circles. First clockwise, then counterclockwise.

Next, stretch your fingers wide. Then make a loose fist. Repeat this movement 3 times.

Bring your arms down and then shake your hands gently at your sides. Feel all that tension from typing, scrolling and just doing office related tasks leaving your body.

Now relax and get into your breathing rhythm once again.

When you are ready, place your right hand on your chair, inhale and lift your left arm overhead.

As you exhale, gently lean to your right.

Let your head drop toward your right shoulder.

Breathe here for 3 full breaths. Come back to the center and then switch sides.

Repeat this routine for at least 2 times on both sides or until you start feeling lighter.

Return to your start position and keep up with the breath work. S

To close the movements for this session, sit on the edge of your seat with your feet slightly apart.

Inhale, then slowly fold your body forward from the hips. Let your arms and head hang downward as you do so.

Stay here for 5 slow breaths before you slowly roll up. Stay here for a few quiet breaths.

Allow your mind to soften. Give yourself permission to let the day fade.

Now, place your hands on your thighs with your palms facing up.

Take a deep breath through your nose and then exhale through your mouth.

As you breathe, repeat these words you are about to hear to yourself

*"I've done enough today. I can rest now."*

Let those words settle in your mind. Allow your body to receive them.

Every time you exhale, imagine stress leaving your body.

And every time you inhale, invite in peace and ease.

Stay here for as long as you need. When you feel ready, slowly open your eyes.

# CHAPTER SEVEN
# FULL DAILY ROUTINE

This last chapter in part of this book is all about giving you options when it comes to real, practical chair yoga. Each of the flows that you find here are designed to fit different moods and moments in your day. Perhaps you have only got a full 15 minutes to recharge or maybe you need something grounding as a work-from-home parent. We created a flow for that exact season. Typically, most people are navigating a high-stress day that has pushed them to the edge. Whichever category you fall into, this chapter meets you right where you are. These flows combine efficient breathwork, mindful movement, and intentional stillness to help you reset with purpose. In this chapter, you can expect to find;

- A 15-minute energizing flow to refresh your body and mind when you have time to spare

- A gentle, nurturing session for work-from-home parents balancing chaos and calm

- A powerful stress relief flow to help you shake off tension and reclaim your focus

Each one is guided and structured in a way that makes it easy for you to follow. You can also customize it to accommodate your needs and time constraints. The flow is efficient yet simple so that you can show up for yourself, breathe through the hassles and put in some movement no matter what kind of day you are having.

# 15-MINUTE CHAIR YOGA FLOW

This session is your chance to reset the proverbial clock. You use this flow on days when you have a little extra time on your hands. It doesn't matter whether you are having a slow morning or maybe you found a rare quiet pocket in your day, you want to take this time to move, breathe and reconnect. It's not going to get you sweaty or leave you breathless but can work your core and muscles while keeping you grounded mentally. The starting point as usual is for you to sit tall in your chair, keep your feet grounded and your spine long. Let your hands rest gently on your thighs. From this position, you are ready to launch into your session.

Right after getting the start position right, your next move is to settle into your breathing.

Close your eyes. Take a deep breath through your nose. Then let the air out fully through your mouth.

Do this breathing routine for two more times. Keep your mind rooted in the moment.

Visualize your feet rooting into the ground and think of your seat as your strong support system.

Now it is time to get into some movement.

On your next inhale, roll your shoulders up to your ears. Then as you exhale, roll them backwards and down.

Repeat this movement for about 5 times.

Then return to the starting position before gently dropping your right ear toward your right shoulder.

Hold this for 2 breaths. Then switch sides and repeat. Visualize the tension melting out of your body as you do so.

Return to start position and then from here, you transition into the seated cat-cow movement.

Place both your hands on your knees.

Then inhale. Arch your back, open your chest and lift your chin as you draw in this breath.

Then as you exhale, round your spine and tuck your chin in towards your chest.

Keep your movements in line with your breath and transition slowly from the cow to cat pose for 5 – 6 rounds.

After your 5th or 6th round, on your next inhale, reach your right arm up above your head and then over it to lean into a side stretch.

Exhale and then return to the start position. As you take your next breath, switch sides and repeat everything you did just now on the left.

Do this movement for at least 3 times on each side. Feel your breath expand your ribs and your body soften, then return to start position

Now, place your right hand on your left knee and your left hand on the chair's back.

Take a deep breath to lengthen your spine. Then as you exhale, twist gently to the left.

Hold your body in this position for 3 – 4 breaths. Come back to the start position, then repeat this entire movement on the right.

Return to start position. Take a break here if you need to.

When you are ready, hold the sides of your chair for support and then extend your right leg straight.

Flex your foot and point your toes first towards you and then away from you.

Lower your leg and repeat the same on the left leg and foot.

Do this for about 6 times on each side.

If you need an energy boost, you lift the opposite arm for each leg.

Return to the starting position and begin reengaging with your breathing.

When you get back in rhythm, move toward the edge of your seat.

Keep your feet wide and then take a deep breath.

As you exhale, fold your body forward and let your arms and head dangle/hang.

Stay in this position for 4 deep breaths. Feel gravity doing the work.

Slowly roll your body back up one vertebra at a time. You are done with movements.

The next move is to circle back to your breath work.

Place your hands on your lap with your palms facing up. If your eyes are open, close then now.

Then take one full breath in... and one long breath out.

Say these words to yourself, "I showed up. I feel better. I am ready" in quiet confidence.

Repeat these words as many times as possible until you believe them.

When you are ready, sit for a few moments in stillness before gently opening your eyes. You are ready!

## GUIDED CHAIR YOGA FLOW FOR SUPER STRESSFUL DAYS

This flow is for those days that you feel like you experience back-to-back pressure with no breathing room. You can't control the chaos but you can definitely limit the impact it has on your physical and mental health. The beauty of chair yoga as we have emphasized in chapters is that it takes you beyond just physical fitness. It is flexible enough to work with your emotional needs, time constraints and physical limitations. This chair yoga flow for super stressful work days is like a full-body sigh that allows you counteract the effects of stress by simply releasing it. It is calming without making you feel sleepy and it makes you feel strong without being pushy. So take a deep breath to get into it.

Sit tall and straight in your chair. Keep your feet flat on the ground and your spine elongated. Let your hands rest gently on your thighs. This is your starting position.

We will start the session with a breathing exercise. Now close your eyes.

Take a deep breath for a count of 4. Hold your breath for a count of 4.

Exhale for a count of 4.

Then hold for a count of 4.

Repeat this breath technique forfour rounds.

Next, inhale and then pull your shoulder blades upwards and together. To really get results, pretend that there is a pencil somewhere at the center above you and you are trying to squeeze it with your shoulders.

Now exhale and let your shoulders drop. Repeat this move 5 times.

This releases tension that may be stored deep in your upper back.

From the starting position, lift both of your arms over your head.

Now grab your left wrist with your right hand.

Inhale and then lengthen your posture.

Then exhale and bend to the right.

Hold this position for 3 breaths.

Return to your start position, switch sides and repeat the movement.

This movement stretches the sides of your body and creates an open space within you for breath and calm.

Do this movement 3 times on each side and then return to your start position.

Next, cross your right ankle over your left thigh. Sit tall and straight.

Now take a deep breath and bend your upper body forward gently. You can hold the sides of your chair for support or let them hang on your sides. Do what feels most natural to you.

Hold this position and then do 5 deep breaths. Feel the air go all the way down to your lower abdomen.

Return to your start position, cross your left ankle over your right thigh and repeat the movements

Repeat this movement 3 times on both sides and then return to your start position.

Next, inhale and raise your arms sideways.

Now exhale and twist your body to the right. Your arms should be wide open when you do this. One arm should be in front and the other one behind.

Inhale as you come back to the center.

Then exhale and twist your body to the left. Repeat this movement 3 times on each side. This helps to reset your spine and refreshes your mental clarity.

If the chair you are using has a long back, then lift your arms all the way up and then follow through on the body twist.

Return to start position, settle into your chair and then on your next inhale, sweep both arms up.

Exhale and then turn palms down before slowly lowering your arms as if you are moving through water.

Repeat this slow movement 4 - 5 times. Feel your breath slow down and your thoughts become steadier with each rep .

Return to your start position when you complete the last rep.

Now place your hands over your heart.

Close your eyes and inhale deeply...follow this with a slow exhale.

Say the following words gently but firmly to yourself;

*"I release what I can't control."*

*"I return to my center."*

Stay in this stillness for a minute, you are good right here. And when you feel ready open your eyes and bask in the warmth surrounding you for a minute before getting back to your work routine.

## BONUS CHAIR YOGA FLOW FOR THE BUSY WORK FROM HOME PARENT

Parenting is a full-time job that can keep you working at odd hours (depending on your home set-up). If you are working a regular job from home in addition to being a parent, it is not surprising to find yourself feeling stretched thin and stressed out with little to no energy. This chair yoga flow is designed to ground your body, open up space in your mind and give you a little soul lift in the middle of the daily chaos. It is gentle, nourishing and meant to feel like a breather in every sense of the word. You might feel a little parental guilt for indulging in this but you have to remind yourself that between the snack preps, emails, video calls and tiny voices calling your name, you have earned this pause. So find your spot, sit tall in your chair, keep your feet grounded with your hands resting softly on your lap and let us begin.

We will start the session by setting your intention. So first, close your eyes.

Next, take a deep breath slowly through your nose...and then exhale gently through your mouth.

Think of your breath as a door that is gently closing on the outside world.

Say these words to yourself

*"I am here. I am safe. I deserve this moment"*

Breathe into these. Let it sink in.

When you feel settled in, you can get into the exercises. You can choose to pause and focus on your breathing here or begin the movements right away.

For the first movement take a deep and then roll your shoulders up toward your ears.

Then slowly exhale and roll them back and down. Do this 3 times.

Next, drop your right ear toward your right shoulder. Hold this position for two slow breaths.

Then return to center, switch sides and repeat. Again, do this 3 times.

When you do this movement, allow your neck to loosen. Let your jaw soften. Feel the weight from whatever tension you might be holding in these areas leave your body.

Return to center and then place both your hands on your knees.

Now take a deep as you arch your back. lift your chest and chin. Say these words quietly to yourself,


*"I welcome energy"*


Then exhale as you round your spine and tuck your chin. Say these words as you do so,


*"I release tension"*

Repeat this process for 5 rounds. Ensure that you sync your breath with words and movement.

Return to your start position and on your next inhale, lift your right arm over your head.

Exhale and stretch gently to your left.

Hold this position for 2 breaths and then come back up to your start.

Put your hand down, switch sides and repeat the movement for at least 5 times on each side.

As you do this move, say these words gently to yourself,

*"I create space for breath, for ease, and for me"*

Return to the starting position and place your right hand on your left knee. Keep your left hand behind you.

On your next inhale, lengthen your upper and then exhale as you gently twist to your left. Hold this position for 3 breaths.

Now return to center, switch sides and repeat this movement for 3 times on each side.

Return to start position. Balance your breathing and align your body for the next movement.

Do a slow march as you sit. Lift one leg up as high as you can and then the other as you bring the previous leg down.

Add a gentle arm lift as you move. This gets the blood flowing and shakes off that fatigue that plagues most working parents.

Repeat for 8–10 rounds at a pace that is comfortable for you.

When you are ready to go into the next movement, return to center and once again, stabilize your breath.

Now sit near the edge of your chair.

Inhale and then fold your upper body forward over your legs.

Let your arms and head hang as you gently exhale.

Keep your breathing here deep and even. Feel your mind and body become lighter with every exhale. Do this for 5 breaths and then return to the starting position.

Repeat until you feel completely light.

Now sit upright again. Keep both your hands on your heart or lap. Close your eyes.

Take a deep breath...let it fill up your chest and all the way down to your belly.

Then exhale slowly...

Now say these words to yourself with as much love and positivity you can muster;


*"I am enough"*

*"I give with love and receive with grace"*

*"I return to my day with calm and presence"*


Take one more deep breath. Exhale as you open your eyes. Stretch if you need to or just sit still and enjoy the way you are feeling in that moment.

# PART THREE:
## STAYING CONSISTENT AND MINDFUL

# CHAPTER EIGHT
# CREATING A SUSTAINABLE HABIT

Part one and part two of this book delved into what chair yoga is about and the practice of chair yoga. This last part is about integrating chair yoga into your daily routine for better results. This chapter is rooted in staying consistent because even the best intentions can fade without the right mindset and strategy. Here, we will explore simple and realistic ways to weave chair yoga into your daily life, even when things get hectic. You will learn how to turn small moments into opportunities for movement as well as how to stay grounded when motivation slips or distractions creep in. Here's a quick look at what you can expect;

- Creative tips for integrating chair yoga into your daily routine at home or work, without needing extra time or space

- Practical guidance on overcoming common obstacles like time pressure, low motivation, and constant distractions

- Insightful strategies for using mindfulness and habit-stacking to build a practice that actually lasts

Think of this chapter as your toolkit for making chair yoga something you do because it works for you, not just because you have to do it.

## HOW TO BUILD CHAIR YOGA INTO YOUR DAILY ROUTINE

Adding chair yoga into your daily routine doesn't have to be something grand or rigid. With a little planning and intentionality, it can actually become one of the most natural yet personalized parts of your day. One creative way to do this is by pairing chair yoga with your already existing habits. For example, while you wait for your morning coffee to brew or your computer to boot up, you can do a few gentle seated stretches or breathwork exercises. When you do it this way, these little moments of stillness or movement become bookmarks in your day that helps your body and mind remember to pause and reset for a better work experience.

Another tip to help you integrate chair yoga into your day is to incorporate sound cues or visual reminders. We touched on this before but the focus then was getting you transition from work to end of day flow. Here, the objective is to inject simple flows into pockets of your day without disrupting your current routine. You can set a soft chime on your phone at a specific time each day. Perhaps mid-morning or just before your afternoon slump. Choose a time when you are most likely to engage as opposed to what people generally assume is ideal. And when that chime goes off, treat it like a personal wellness alert. Your time for two minutes of breathwork or a quick chair twist. Reframing it this way takes the pressure off you making it easier for you to participate.

You can also place a sticky note on your monitor with a short reminder like, "Breathe + Stretch," or use calming desktop wallpapers as subtle prompts. These cues serve as breaks in your work day and they help you to create a new rhythm that keeps your body from falling into static stress patterns. Lastly, make chair yoga something you look forward to by adding a personal touch to it. If you have practiced enough to have your own flow memorized, you can use a favorite playlist during your stretch. Another cool thing is to keep a light essential oil nearby for calming sensory support. That scent personalizes your routine and helps to affirm the moment as your time.

The truth is you don't have to carve out a big chunk of time to get the most out of your chair yoga sessions. Instead, build micro-sessions that are centered around your energy and emotional needs each day. With these tiny steps, your chair yoga sessions can slip in like a quiet act of self-care. If you tie your practice sessions to moments of gratitude or self-reflection, you can reshape your attitude towards your chair yoga practice.

## OVERCOMING OBSTACLES: TIME, MOTIVATION, DISTRACTIONS

Chair yoga is great as we have already mentioned. But getting into consistent practice doesn't come without it's own set of challenges. Being aware of what you are up against can help you to be mentally prepared to handle it. One of the biggest challenges most people talk about is time or more accurately, the feeling of never having enough of it. Thankfully, you don't need a 30-minute time block to get the benefits. Even one or two minutes of movement or deep breathing is enough to create a mental reset. So instead of chasing time to practice, start by identifying natural pauses in your day. Use those moments for a quick stretch or calming breath. When you look at chair yoga as something you sprinkle into your routine rather than something you have to actively "make time for," it becomes easier to be consistent at it.

Staying motivated enough to be consistent is another hurdle that many people face. Especially when life gets hectic or you are just not in the mood to do any kind of workout. One way to keep your practice alive is by attaching it to something meaningful. Earlier on, we talked about reframing. So instead of thinking of it as just exercise, see it as your permission slip to pause or your personal act of reclaiming a little peace. You can take things a step further by keeping a simple tracker or journal where you jot down how you feel after each session. Over time, these notes become reminders that every little effort adds up and actually makes your day better.

Lastly, you have to deal with distractions. Even the best intentions can get derailed if you don't manage your distractions. There are tons of distractions at home and at work that can keep you from following through on your yoga practice. The first one is general noise. If you are in a position where you can't escape the noise, try shutting it out by using headphones, a calming playlist or guided audio flows. Another thing you can do is let family or coworkers know you are taking a short wellness break and then, honor that space like you would any other important task. People tend to follow your cues. If you can't escape the noise, embrace it. In truth, chair yoga doesn't demand absolute silence for practice. It would be ideal but it is adaptive. What matters the most is your attention. With enough practice, you will eventually learn how to center yourself even in the midst of noise or chaos.

## USING MINDFULNESS AND HABIT-STACKING

Mindfulness is a powerful tool that you can use to make your chair yoga practice stick. Most people tend to get into the practice of chair yoga by including it on their to do list. This is not entirely ineffective but for long term, it might not be sustainable. So rather than thinking of yoga as a chore to check off a list, approach it with presence. A part of that means being observant of how your breath feels as you move, where tension lives in your body and how even a small stretch shifts your mood. Over time, you will begin to associate chair yoga practice with calmness, focus and clarity. This creates a positive reinforcement that makes you want to come back to it, not just because you should or because you are supposed to but because you actually feel better when you do.

Habit-stacking on the other hand is a simple method for fitting chair yoga into a busy day without overthinking it. The general idea is to attach your chair yoga practice to an existing habit so it becomes automatic. What that could look like could be you doing two minutes of breathwork right after brushing your teeth or maybe stretching your arms and spine each time you refill your coffee cup. These small simple pairings help build consistency, because you are not starting from scratch. You are building on something that you already do. In time, it becomes second nature, like muscle memory for your routine.

Combining mindfulness and habit-stacking turns chair yoga into a natural part of your day rather than a forced task. You find yourself moving with more awareness, breathing with intention and slowly creating small rituals that ground you. This could show up as a mindful twist after checking emails or a deep breath before your first meeting. These little choices help you build a habit that's not only doable, but deeply nurturing. It becomes less about finding time and more about shaping your day around what helps you feel whole.

# CHAPTER NINE
# CHAIR YOGA AT WORK

This chapter focuses on how you can bring chair yoga into shared spaces and group settings in a way that's fun, practical and easy to adopt. While it is nice for you to get into your daily chair yoga routine and do your thing, creating an environment that values and encourages movements can make it even more beneficial. This chapter offers creative ways to make chair yoga a group-friendly experience. Here you will learn how to turn everyday moments into opportunities for wellness without disrupting routines. Here are some of the things that you will explore;

● Creative ways to use chair yoga during meetings, breaks, and between tasks to stay grounded and focused

● Simple, office-friendly stretches that work in both formal and relaxed environments without drawing attention

● Tips to encourage group participation in chair yoga whether you are in a workplace, on a virtual team or sharing space at home

Going forward, it is all about weaving wellness into your day and inviting others to do the same.

## HOW TO USE CHAIR YOGA IN MEETINGS, DURING BREAKS, AND IN BETWEEN TASKS

The thought of doing chair yoga during meetings might sound strange at first, but it can present an opportunity to stay grounded and engaged especially when you have one of those long virtual calls. You don't have to go for anything elaborate. Do something as simple as keeping your feet flat and your spine long as you sit in your chair. You can also try keeping your focus on your posture as you listen to this call. Whenever you are muted, you can gently roll your shoulders, do seated pelvic tilts or softly press your hands together in a calming mudra. These micro-movements not only reduce stiffness but also improve focus and presence. For those meetings that feel like they are going on forever, especially ones where you are mostly listening, you can alternate between deep nasal breathing with subtle stretches to keep your energy calm but alert.

Breaks while you are working offers you the perfect window to reset with chair yoga. As you already know, no fancy setup is needed. You just need to be more intentional. So instead of reaching for your phone or grabbing another snack, use 3–5 minutes to re-energize. Try doing a seated backbend by placing your hands behind the chair and lifting your chest, or stretch your wrists and fingers to relieve tension from typing. You can also try mindful blinking or palming the eyes to soothe visual fatigue that comes from staring at your screen for too long. Pair any of this with a few gentle head circles or a mini seated sun salutation and your entire system will feel refreshed without breaking a sweat.

Between tasks is another overlooked moment where you can skip in some chair yoga practice. The benefit is that it can make a whole lot of difference. Transitioning from one mental task to another like emails to brainstorming can be smoother when you take a moment to reset your body. Try a quick seated twist to reset your spine or do a gentle breath hold (inhale, hold for 4 counts, exhale) to calm your nervous system. Even lifting your arms over your head and breathing deeply can act as a mental reset button. The idea is to use these moments of transition not as empty meaningless pauses, but as small intentional rituals that refresh your body and sharpen your focus for whatever comes next.

## OFFICE-FRIENDLY STRETCHES

Since habit stacking is highly encouraged, you want to look at movements that you can do while you carry out certain tasks or in between tasks. The office-friendly stretches we talk about here are designed to be subtle, effective and easy to do without drawing too much attention. One great stretch is the upper back opener. Basically, you clasp your hands together in front of you, push your palms outward and then gently round your upper back as if creating space between your shoulder blades. This move helps to relieve tightness from sitting in a forward-leaning position. It also gives your spine a refreshing relief as you curve in the opposite direction. You can do this seated right at your desk while staying fully engaged in your workspace.

Another office friendly stretch is the seated figure four position which we have talked about. This is particularly useful if you tend to sit for long hours. To get into this movement, cross your right ankle over your left knee to form a figure four shape. Sit tall, and if it feels okay, lean forward slightly to deepen the stretch in your hip. Hold for a few breaths and then switch sides. It looks relaxed and casual but does powerful work in releasing tension in the lower body. If your work culture is more formal, you can keep things subtle by adjusting your position so that you are not too obvious and then add small seated pelvic tilts.

Lastly, we have the chin tuck and neck glide. This stretch is exactly what it says it is and can be done right in front of a screen without needing to move your chair. Start by sitting upright, then gently pull your chin straight back (like you're making a double chin). Hold for a few seconds and then release. Repeat this slowly several times to realign the head and neck. This helps reduce the negative impact of the forward-head posture which is a common issue with desk jobs. Follow this movement up with soft side-to-side head turns or even jaw circles to loosen up the muscles that often go stiff when you are deep in concentration. These movements help improve posture and reduce tension without needing to step away from your desk or disrupt your workflow.

## Encouraging Team Participation

Getting other people on board with chair yoga can be a fun way to build a more relaxed and connected environment. This rings true whether you are in a workplace or working from home with family or roommates. One creative approach is to introduce a "movement minute" at the start or end of a group meeting. You don't need to lead a full session. Just a simple stretch, deep breath or even a wrist roll can serve as a shared mental reset. When this becomes part of the meeting routine, people begin to expect and appreciate that brief pause, especially when it helps them feel more focused.

Another great way to boost participation is by turning the experience into a game. Create a weekly "movement challenge" where team members pick a chair yoga pose to practice and share feedback, photos, or short clips (if appropriate). At home, turn it into a lighthearted family ritual where everyone joins in for a few moments of stretching after lunch or before bed. Adding this game element to it takes the pressure off and helps people see chair yoga as accessible rather than something formal or intimidating.

In a more structured environment when you are not exactly influential, you can subtly get your co-workers on board by tying your chair yoga practice to shared goals like better focus, less tension or improved posture. Share your experience casually in informal settings. Mention how a two-minute twist helped you reset before a tough task or how you feel less stiff at the end of the day. Whenever anyone complains about stress, work frustration or some posture related pain, encourage them to try out a few chair yoga poses. If you are working remotely, consider hosting a virtual chair yoga break once a week or sharing a short guided video. That said, if you want their participation, you want to keep it light, consistent and most importantly, pressure-free. Over time, people would naturally become more curious and open when they see real benefits in someone else's routine.

# CHAPTER TEN
# CHAIR YOGA FOR DIFFERENT NEEDS

This chapter is all about making chair yoga work for you regardless of your age, ability or experience level. This chapter explores how to shape your chair yoga practice to meet your body's needs and your lifestyle by offering thoughtful ways to adapt, simplify or deepen your routine. Whether you are brand new, easing into movement after a long break or simply looking for something that feels more personal, this chapter gives you the tools to move with confidence and care. Here's what you will find as you move forward:

- Creative tips for customizing chair yoga for stress relief, posture support, and mental clarity.

- Gentle, thoughtful approaches to practicing chair yoga for seniors, beginners, and those with limited mobility.

- Encouragement to build a routine that honors your unique pace, preferences, and physical comfort.

It is a known fact that no two bodies are alike and there's no reason for your yoga experience to be like everyone else's. No matter where you are on your journey, this chapter is your reminder that small movements, done mindfully, can lead to big shifts in how you feel every day.

## CUSTOMIZING YOUR PRACTICE: FOR STRESS RELIEF, POSTURE CORRECTION, MENTAL CLARITY

One of the many benefits of chair yoga practice is how adaptive it is to your needs. We have shared movements and created chair yoga flows to get you started. But to take things a step further, you want to be able to adapt it to meet you where you are and this means learning to create flows that work for when you are stressed, suffering from poor posture or just needing some mental clarity when you are in the middle of chaos. So let's start with stress. Customizing your chair yoga practice for stress relief starts with you being able to identify your personal stress signals. This could be tight shoulders, shallow breath and/or racing thoughts. The next step is to tailor your flow to calm those areas. In this case, you start with grounding breathwork, then build in stretches that directly release where you feel the most tension. For example, if you carry stress in your chest or upper back, use seated heart openers and shoulder sweeps. If your mind won't slow down, incorporate longer exhalations and forward folds. You can also personalize your practice by setting a calming intention or using soft music or aromatherapy to shift your mood before you begin.

When your focus is posture correction, you have to build your flow around spinal alignment and awareness for better results. Start with gentle core engagement. Chair yoga forms like seated pelvic tilts or pressing your feet firmly into the floor as you lengthen your spine can be very useful here. You can also add in seated cat-cow movements, chin tucks, and shoulder blade retraction to retrain your muscles to support better posture. You could even place a small pillow or rolled towel behind your lower back to help maintain natural spinal curves while you practice. Visual cues like sitting tall as if you are balancing a book on your head can also keep you mindful of your alignment throughout the day.

To boost mental clarity, the most efficient practice is to blend breathwork with simple, repetitive movements that synchronize with your inhales and exhales. Do gentle arm lifts paired with slow breathing or rhythmic seated twists help recenter your thoughts and improve focus. To take things another step further, you can also incorporate visualizations like imagining each inhale bringing in clarity and each exhale releasing mental clutter. For deeper clarity, try a short seated meditation after your flow. Focusing on a single word or affirmation like "***focus***" or "***ease***" can amplify the impact of your meditation session and this works to keep your mind steady, especially during high-pressure moments or when you need to transition from one task to the next with calm intention.

## Tips for Seniors, People with Limited Mobility, and Beginners

Chair yoga can be practiced at any level. You just need to be cognizant of where you are in terms of fitness, acknowledge your limitations and then work with them. Practicing chair yoga as a senior is all about choosing movements that feel safe and supportive while boosting your confidence. Before you even begin a session, using props like cushions or rolled towels to support your back or knees during seated postures can make a difference. Gentle movements such as ankle rolls, wrist circles and slow head turns can be deeply effective without requiring much effort. Doing your sessions near a sturdy table or wall adds extra stability and peace of mind. Seniors can also benefit from shorter, more frequent sessions. So instead of doing a longer session all at once, aim for a few minutes of movement throughout the day.

If you are dealing with limited mobility, customization is key. It is helpful (and practical ) to focus on areas that can move freely, instead of trying to force a full-body routine. For example, hand mudras, facial movements and deep breathing exercises can be practiced entirely from a seated or reclined position. You get the benefits without putting unnecessary physical strain on your body. Visualization can also enhance the experience. When you are deep into a session, imagining yourself moving with ease can help stimulate neural connections and support gentle mobility over time. To create an inviting space that encourages regular practice without pressure, use soft, supportive lighting and calming background sounds.

As for beginners, it is not uncommon to feel unsure about where to start. The key to getting into the swing of things is keeping it simple and consistent. Rather than diving into a full 30-minute practice packed with several forms, choose 3–5 basic movements to begin with and repeat them daily until they feel familiar. Breathing techniques like simple diaphragmatic breathing can be a starting point before introducing physical movement. As a beginner, you should also feel empowered to adapt each movement to your own pace and comfort level. Watching or listening to guided sessions can help you to build your confidence. Journaling afterward even if you are just noting how your body feels can create awareness and motivation. With time, these small steps lead to a strong, supportive practice that meets your body exactly where it is, without needing to "catch up" to anyone else.

# CONCLUSION

Hey, you made it! All the way to the end. That is no small feat especially in a world that pulls your attention in a hundred directions at once. The fact that you carved out the time no matter how long the process took you... to learn how to reconnect with your breath, your body and your center through chair yoga means you have already taken the most important step. You have proven to yourself that self-care can be simple, that movement doesn't have to be loud to be powerful and that even in the busiest of days, you can still choose peace.

Take a moment to reflect on how far you have come. Maybe your posture feels a little taller now. Maybe your mind is just a touch quieter. Maybe you have found new ways to meet yourself with kindness in the middle of your daily hustle. No matter how small the milestone, celebrate it. That is the real magic of chair yoga. It meets you where you are and grows with you. You didn't need a studio, a mat, or a lifestyle overhaul. Just a chair. Just a breath. Just you showing up.

All that being said, this isn't the end of your journey. It is only the beginning. The real transformation you want happens in those small, everyday decisions you make to pause, to move, to breathe. Keep your chair yoga practice alive by making it your own. Make it playful when you need joy. Make it grounding when you feel overwhelmed. Make it consistent, not because you have to, but because you want to feel good in your body and mind. That is the secret to keep going long after you close this book.

As you carry this practice forward, hold onto this final mindfulness message. You don't have to be perfect, you only have to be present.

Being present, being aware and being fully intentional is the true heart of yoga. Remind yourself as often as you need to that you are enough, exactly as you are. Any image of perfection that you hold on to can serve as inspiration but never use it as a milestone for your mental, physical and emotional well-being. The person you are right now, who shows up for every session, who prioritizes simple movements throughout the day deserves to be happy right now. You are powerful and every breath you take in that truth deepens your strength and your stillness.

To wrap things up, here's your closing affirmation. Say it with pride and mean it; *"I honor my body. I trust my breath. I return to myself, again and again"*. Keep showing up. Keep moving with intention. You can do this!

# THANK YOU FOR PRACTICING WITH ME

**Enjoyed these calming Chair Yoga routines?**

I'm so glad!

You can find more wellness tips, resources,
and updates here:

## www.theawesomereaders.com

Stay grounded, stay inspired — one breath at a time.

— Aria Sage